W0247018

the little book of
CRYSTAL
HEALING

Copyright © 2024 Headline Publishing Group

The right of Katalin Németh to be identified as the Author of the Work has been asserted by her in accordance with the Copyright, Designs and Patents Act 1988.

First published in 2024 by OH
An Imprint of HEADLINE PUBLISHING GROUP

1

Disclaimer:

This book is intended for general informational purposes only and should not be relied upon as recommending or promoting any specific practice, diet or method of treatment. It is not intended to diagnose, advise, treat or prevent any illness or condition and is not a substitute for advice from a professional practitioner of the subject matter contained in this book. You should not use the information in this book as a substitute for medication, nutritional, diet, spiritual or other treatment that is prescribed by your practitioner. Furthermore, the publisher is not affiliated with and does not sponsor or endorse any uses of or beliefs about in any way referred in this book.

Apart from any use permitted under UK copyright law, this publication may only be reproduced, stored, or transmitted, in any form, or by any means, with prior permission in writing of the publishers or, in the case of reprographic production, in accordance with the terms of licences issued by the Copyright Licensing Agency.

Cataloguing in Publication Data is available from the British Library

ISBN 978-1-03541-968-5

Compiled and written by: Katalin Németh
Editorial: Saneaah Muhammad
Designed and typeset in Joanna Sans Nova by: Andy Jones
Project manager: Russell Porter
Illustrations: Freepik.com
Production: Rachel Burgess
Printed and bound in China

MIX
Paper | Supporting
responsible forestry
FSC® C104740

Headline's policy is to use papers that are natural, renewable and recyclable products and made from wood grown in well-managed forests and other controlled sources. The logging and manufacturing processes are expected to conform to the environmental regulations of the country of origin.

HEADLINE PUBLISHING GROUP
An Hachette UK Company
Carmelite House, 50 Victoria Embankment, London EC4Y 0DZ

www.headline.co.uk   www.hachette.co.uk

the little book of
CRYSTAL
HEALING

katalin németh

CONTENTS

Chapter 5

How to Work With
the Chakras   76

Chapter 6

Most Commonly
Used Crystals   86

Chapter 7

Crystal Combinations
for Specific Ailments   184

CHAPTER

1

WHAT are CRYSTALS and HOW DO THEY WORK?

Crystals are a solid form of matter, with their atoms arranged into highly ordered patterns. Each type of crystal has a unique structural pattern that gives it distinct healing powers.

Everything in this universe is made up of vibrations: light, sound and even matter. Crystals work by emanating beneficial and healing vibrations.

Crystals make use of these vibrations by lending them to the human body when they come into contact with it, helping it to rebalance and heal itself.

Crystals can also share these vibrations with other living organisms, such as animals and plants, and with non-living things similar to themselves, such as water.

Humankind has used crystals since the dawn of time. These beautiful stones have served as decorations, signs of power and as healing and ritualistic items.

The healing properties listed in this book draw from the practices of many generations of healers who have worked with crystals and learned about their unique powers.

It is not a coincidence that the ancient Sumerians, Incas, Egyptians and Indians all used lapis lazuli for their royal headdresses and accessories.

These ancient civilizations also discovered the power of many other crystals, such as jade, turquoise, carnelian and amber.

Use crystal healing as a complementary therapy alongside your existing form of healing.

Although crystals are potent healers, some ailments call for conventional medical treatment or advice from a medical professional.

CHAPTER

2

HOW to CHOOSE your CRYSTALS

There are hundreds of types of crystal that can be collected, all with different colours, shapes and sizes. It may seem daunting to start your collection, but as with all things in life, it's okay to begin one step, or crystal, at a time.

Every crystal has a specific healing property that sets it apart from the rest. While many crystals have similar properties and effects, the feeling that each one provides to the individual is distinct from the others.

To choose your healing crystals, search for the different crystals that might provide the specific healing you are in need of. Decide on its shape and size and how you will implement it in your everyday life – for example as a necklace, a feng shui piece or a palm stone.

Once you have narrowed down the crystals that might work for you, you have a starting point for your collection! It is best to search for your crystals in spaces and stores where you are able to see and feel them – and where crystal experts are present to provide more details about each crystal.

If you feel overwhelmed by the selection of crystals, take a step back and allow yourself a moment to study each of them. There is often one crystal that you will feel drawn to – hold this crystal, close your eyes and allow yourself to sense its energy. If the crystal is meant for you, you're likely to feel a positive sensation, such as a soft buzzing, warmth, peace or joy.

If you aren't sensitive to subtle energies, choose the one you like the most based on its looks. For example, to help with anxiety, you could choose a moonstone pendant.

It's okay if you aren't sensitive to subtle energies – you can still find the crystal that is right for you. A crystal can often stand out to an individual simply by the way it looks or by the way you feel inside when the crystal is near.

It's always important to collect crystals from ethical sources, to be mindful of both the environment and those who mine the crystals.

WHAT SIZE?

The size of the specimen
will depend on what you
want to use it for.

Jewellery is a beautiful way to adorn or wear a crystal, and necklaces are a common choice. 1–2 cm specimens are the perfect size to use as pendants, or you can opt for a "cage" or locket, which allows you to change the crystal that sits within.

Some crystals, such as lapis lazuli or moldavite, are very potent and should be used in limited quantities or small sizes in order to contain their effects. These small crystals can be designed as rings or earrings, but should be worn sparingly.

Tumbled crystals can be carried in little pouches, perfect to keep with you on the go.

For chakra healing and meditation, palm stones of about 5 cm and bigger are a good choice. Their smooth surface makes them really pleasant to hold, and they are big enough for to emanate the strong vibrations you need.

You can also use small clusters, wands or specially carved shapes for this purpose.

For enhancing a room's vibrations, bigger clusters, geodes or carvings of 10 cm and bigger are recommended, if you can afford them, but a bunch of smaller specimens kept together can also work fine.

WHAT SHAPE?

The shape of a specimen can enhance its healing powers by directing its energy in a specific way.

tumbled stones and crystals are small, shiny specimens. They are portable, affordable, very versatile and usually in their natural shape.

They can be used for creating grids and mandalas, chakra healing and meditating or to wear as jewellery or keep on a keyring; the possibilities are endless.

palm stones are usually flat, oval-shaped stones and crystals that have been shaped for the purpose of holding in your hand. They can also be placed at any point of the body that you want to heal, especially on the main chakras.

single-point crystals are great as wands and pendulums. Energy will flow into whichever direction the point is facing. They are great for healing a specific area of the body or for cleansing and re-energizing other crystals.

double-point crystals are great for balancing out energy, leading negative energy out and ushering positive energy in at the same time.

clusters and geodes are great for energizing rooms or for cleansing smaller crystals.

pyramid-shaped crystals

are conductors of positive energy and represent ancient knowledge and sacred geometry.

egg- and sphere-shaped crystals are often used as crystal balls

for fortune telling, especially if they are made of clear quartz.

They can be used to energize rooms and to meditate.

hearts, skulls, crosses, angels and animals carved from crystals can help you to connect to the archetypical energies that they represent, such as love, knowledge, faith, spirit guides or the attributes that different animals are associated with.

They can be used like any other crystal, depending on their size.

BIRTH
STONES

There are two ways in which crystals are assigned as birth stones: according to your Sun zodiac sign or according to your month of birth. As both lists are similar, we have combined them into one.

Birthstones are especially potent for people with corresponding zodiac signs, so if you are torn between buying two crystals and one falls into the list of your birth stones, you might want to choose that one.

aries
Garnet, carnelian, clear quartz, blood stone.

taurus
Emerald, malachite, rose quartz, selenite.

gemini
Pearl, agate, citrine, tiger's eye.

cancer
Ruby, agate, moonstone.

leo
Onyx, amber, sunstone, ruby.

virgo
Peridot, smithsonite, amazonite.

libra
Sapphire, obsidian, citrine, blood stone.

scorpio
Topaz, peridot, ruby, labradorite, malachite, turquoise.

sagittarius
Citrine, lapis lazuli, obsidian, amethyst.

capricorn
Garnet, tiger's eye, smoky quartz, tourmaline.

aquarius
Aquamarine, amber, angelite, amethyst.

pisces
Amethyst, lepidolite, aquamarine, lapis lazuli.

CHAPTER

3

HOW to WORK with CRYSTALS

CLEANSING

There are many ways to cleanse your crystals, and they all work equally well.

The only thing to keep in mind is the structure of the crystal, because some might dissolve in water or become discoloured under the Sun.

Always consult your crystal seller if you are unsure, but the following four ways should work with any crystal, regardless of how porous it is.

How frequently you need to cleanse your crystals will depend on how you use them. If a crystal is used intensely and daily, like a necklace you are continuously wearing, it will likely need daily cleansing.

A crystal used for healing multiple people consecutively must be cleansed between each session.

If you only use the crystal occasionally or as a static item – such as a big cluster used to energize a room – then it can be cleansed and reprogrammed weekly or even monthly.

Use your intuition to determine how often it should happen, but always try to cleanse your crystal before it gathers dust.

SMUDGING

Smudging, or smoke cleansing, is one of the best ways to cleanse crystals.

Light a bunch of sage, bay leaves or even your favourite incense sticks, and use them to cleanse your crystals by bathing them in smoke and willing any residual energy to leave.

Open all the windows in the room, so any negative energy has a way to leave.

WATER

Most crystals are suitable for being cleansed with water.

Take caution and check if water is safe for your crystal, because it could damage the shine on the surface or even cause deeper damage by releasing potentially toxic, carcinogen elements that make up the crystal.

A good rule of thumb is to remember that if a crystal ends with -ite (e.g., selenite, malachite or hematite), it should not be submerged in water, though there are also some other exceptions that should not be soaked or left in water.

A safe way to cleanse most crystals is to carefully dab them with a wet cloth.

Take a clean cotton cloth and hold it under the tap or submerse it in moon water. Dab your crystal clean with the wet cloth and then gently pat the crystal dry with a soft towel used specifically for your crystals.

MOON BATHING

For crystals that you have had for some time and have already cleansed at least once with either of the two previous methods, moon bathing is a great option.

On the night of the full moon, leave the crystal outside on a table or by a window that gets direct moonlight. The gentle light will cleanse and energize the crystal, ready to be used again.

SUN BATHING

Sun bathing works similarly, but if you use this method, you need to be mindful that some crystals might become discoloured by extended exposure to the Sun.

A muslin cloth can be used to cover the crystal to protect it from the Sun while it is cleansing and recharging.

remember:

Clear quartz of any shape, especially clear quartz crystal balls, should never be left in the Sun or by a window that receives sunlight because it could catch the Sun's rays, amplify them like a magnifying glass and cause a fire.

Other methods of cleansing include burying the crystal in the ground or using sound-cleansing, such as bells or singing bowls.

Some of these methods will not be safe for all crystals, so do your research before trying them out.

HOW to PROGRAM a CRYSTAL

After cleansing your crystal, you need to program it. This is to fill the crystal with your intention to use it as a healing tool for a specific purpose.

It is best to use different crystals for different purposes, but you can also program a single crystal to have multiple abilites. You can change the program any time; just cleanse the crystal from its original program and start afresh.

To program a crystal, begin by relaxing into a meditative state. Remain calm and focused. Hold the crystal in your hands and concentrate on the task you want to give to it. Say the task out loud three times, directing your words to the crystal.

As an example, if you want an onyx tumble stone to stay in your bag and protect you when you are out and about, you could say:

"Thank you for protecting me from negative energy by grounding me and reminding me of my own strength."

Or, if you want a carnelian palm stone to help improve your blood circulation, you might say:

"Thank you, dear carnelian, for improving my blood circulation!"

HOW to CREATE an ELIXIR

Infusing water with a crystal's vibrations can be really beneficial. However, you need to keep in mind that water can dissolve carcinogens from some crystals.

Instead of submerging your crystals in water, a safer option for your crystals would be to arrange them around a cup or jug of water, or to cover your container with a lid and place the crystals on top of it.

Using a glass container and lid is a great way to program your water because glass is non-toxic and inert, meaning that it won't react with the crystals or alter the elixir's properties. You can even create grids and mandalas on top of the lid, thereby amplifying the effect of the crystals.

To program your water and create an elixir, pour clear water in a jug, and keep it on a solid surface where it won't be disturbed.

Keep your crystal next to or on top of the jug, and state its purpose, just like when you programmed the crystal.

Say it out loud three times, while holding the jug with your left hand, and keeping the crystal in your right hand. Allow the crystal and water to rest alone for at least an hour, or overnight, when they can also utilize the Moon's healing rays.

When this is done, you can use this water in a number of ways. Drinking a sip every now and then throughout the day will keep you energized and topped up with the crystal's vibrations.

Mixing the elixir with your bath water is an excellent remedy for skin conditions and adding it to your cooking gives your food an extra punch of energy that your whole family can enjoy.

Spraying it around you cleanses the energy of the space and feeding it to your plants also gives them a lovely boost of energy.

Don't forget: never ingest any crystals. They are strictly for external use only.

HOW to
BUILD
a GRID

A crystal grid can be as simple as a cross made of five crystals, or it can be a complicated arrangement using a sacred geometry pattern, such as the Sri Yantra, or the Flower of Life.

For beginners, simpler grids are recommended because the fewer crystals there are, the easier it is to focus your intention.

As you keep practising laying grids, you might want to experiment with more complicated designs for more nuanced results.

You can draw your grid on a piece of paper or paint it on a ceremonial plate. Many grid patterns are available online.

Most importantly, the grid should hold the crystals in place and you should be able to keep it in a safe place where it will not be disturbed.

The time frame a crystal grid needs to complete its task depends greatly on what you want it to manifest.

Relieving a headache might take minutes, whereas aiding recovery from a serious illness could take weeks, or longer.

Nevertheless, as soon as you set up your grid, you can be assured that it has started working towards your goal.

FOLLOW THESE STEPS TO BUILD YOUR GRID:

step 1

Decide what you want your crystal grid to do, then decide on the crystals that will work best.

You will find recommendations for combinations in chapter 6, which lists the most commonly used crystals (see page 86).

Cleanse and program the crystals before laying them out.

step 2

Choose your outline. A cross, a spiral,
a Flower of Life; every template has a
specific meaning that can enhance
your grid.

step 3

Arrange your crystals on the grid.
Start from the outside and progress
inwards toward the central stone. The
centre piece represents your goal of the
grid; the crystals surrounding it provide
help to achieve that goal.

step 4

Activate your grid by touching each crystal on the final grid and speaking its purpose out loud. You can do this with your bare hand or with a crystal point or wand.

step 5

Place your grid in a safe place and let it work. When your goal has been achieved, thank the crystals on it for their help. You can then dismantle the grid and cleanse the crystals.

CHAPTER

4

HOW to use CRYSTALS in MEDITATION

Meditating with crystals can bring emotional healing, energize you for specific tasks and improve your mental health.

Before you begin meditating, carve out some time for your practice when you are free from all distractions, including phone calls, messages, hunger and thirst, other people and pets, etc. Dedicate this time to yourself.

Begin by setting your intention and deciding what you'd like to achieve by meditating with crystals. Is your aim to relieve stress, enhance your psychic abilities, to heal an illness or something else?

Once you have an intention in mind, select the crystal that corresponds to your needs and then cleanse and program it.

How long you meditate depends on your experience level and your technique. For beginners, five minutes is plenty, whereas a more experienced person might meditate for hours. If you have trouble staying on task, and you catch your mind wandering, you could use guided meditation recordings.

Holding the crystal to the point of your body that you'd like to heal while you meditate will also bring about physical benefits.

Settle into a comfortable position – the lotus pose is a wonderful option to allow energy to flow through your chakras (see chapter 5).

The goal is to feel comfortable enough to fall away from the sensation of your body and connect wholly on the crystal in your hand.

Close your eyes and imagine yourself surrounded by the crystal's energy. Begin a breathing exercise by holding this feeling for eight deep breaths.

Breathe in slowly through your nose, envisioning positive energy entering your body and spreading through you with the breath.

Breathe out slowly through your mouth, allowing negative energy, stress and worries to exit your body through your breath.

With each breath you become more and more relaxed.

Remember the instructions of this breathing exercise to use in all aspects of your life when you need to calm your senses, feel more in tune with your body and allow your mind, heart and soul to open up to receiving.

In your mind's eye, visualize your stone in front of you. Let it guide you through the meditation without resisting.

Through the meditation, you may see many different signs. The crystal may show your freedom through the sky, it may invite you to face your shadow self within or it may even show you colours representing emotions and traumas.

Whatever you see, trust your intuition for it to be the exact thing you need at the moment.

Your mind may also take a more silent route, with no thoughts or visuals at all, or you may find it difficult to concentrate. Each practice will allow you to feel more at ease and more in tune with the meditation, the crystal and yourself.

Know that even if you feel nothing at all, you still receive the benefits of the crystal just by spending time with it.

some

EXAMPLES

for a

MEDITATION

SEQUENCE

Meditating with crystals is often practised by using intuition; however, there are also sequences to follow if you are uncertain.

Feel free to use these examples, or to write your own guided meditation based on these.

to enhance your psychic abilities you could consider meditating with lapis lazuli, clear quartz or labradorite.

Hold one of these crystals in your left hand and cover it with your right hand, or place the crystal on your forehead or on top of your head.

Begin with the breathing exercise (see pages 64–65) and imagine the crystal floating in front of you, surrounded by bright white light. Remind yourself that the crystal has the ability to unlock or enhance your psychic abilities.

Let the crystal embrace you with its energy and thank it for its help. Be ready to receive any message that the crystal or your spirit guide has for you.

Call on your spirit guide, and ask for their blessing. Visualize them holding your crystal and touching it to your forehead, where your Third Eye chakra sits, and filling you with the crystal's power. Hear what they have to say, then thank them for coming to your aid.

Slowly bring yourself back to the here and now, and spend some time ruminating about your experience. You may feel or see results immediately, or possibly even years later, when the time is right.

to ease a headache you could consider meditating with angelite, charoite or labradorite.

This meditation is best done lying down, to let the muscles in your neck relax and to reduce any unnecessary tension.

Place the crystal against the painful area of the headache or near to your head, such as on your bedside table or under your pillow.

Begin with the breathing exercise and imagine the crystal floating in front of you.

Visualize the crystal surrounded by bright white light and believe that it has the ability to cure your headache. Let it embrace you with its energy and thank it for its help.

Now visualize your headache as a big ball of dark yarn inside your skull taking up all the space and hurting your head.

Begin unravelling the yarn in your mind by pulling one edge of the string, and watch it leave your head through your Third Eye chakra. Visualize tying the yarn to your crystal and watch the the crystal slowly start to spin, unraveling more and more of the headache out of your head and wrapping it around itself.

As a ball starts to form around the crystal, your headache will reduce and then cease to exist completely when all the yarn has disappeared from your mind.

Now visualize the crystal starting to glow and incinerating the yarn around it, making it impossible for the headache to return.

Thank the crystal for its help, and slowly bring yourself back to the here and now. Spend some time ruminating about your experience. Make a journal entry about how you felt before and how you feel now.

Drink plenty of water and eat something healthy to restore your energy.

CHAPTER

5

HOW to WORK with the CHAKRAS

Chakra healing is beneficial for the whole body. If energy flows unhindered between the chakras, it results in good overall physical and mental health.

If there is an energy blockage, or one of the chakras is overly active, this can lead to physical and mental issues.

To avoid this happening, you can balance your chakras using crystals.

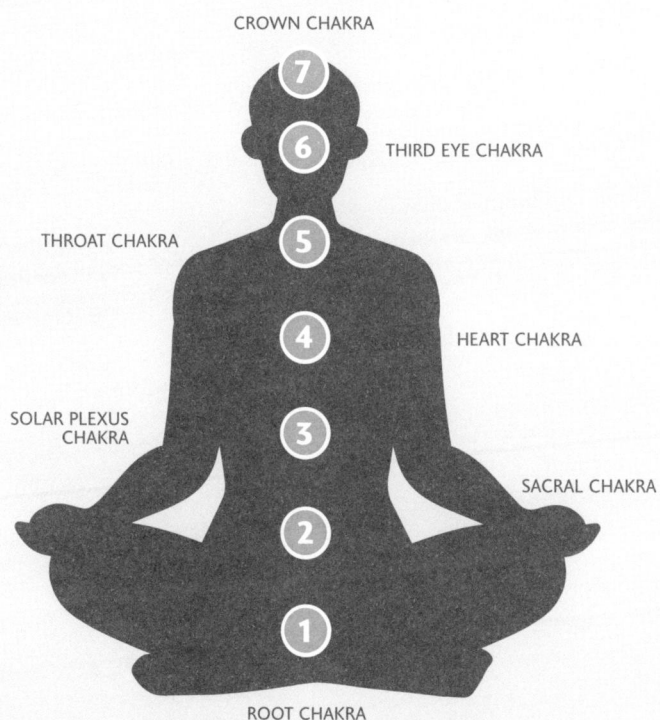

CROWN CHAKRA

THIRD EYE CHAKRA

THROAT CHAKRA

HEART CHAKRA

SOLAR PLEXUS
CHAKRA

SACRAL CHAKRA

ROOT CHAKRA

The chakras and the crystals associated with them are:

ROOT CHAKRA

Black obsidian, onyx, smoky quartz, tourmaline, carnelian, red jasper, rhodochrosite.

The crystal for the Root chakra can go on top of your pubic bone (pubis), between your legs on the bed, or below your tail bone (coccyx).

SACRAL CHAKRA

Amber, sunstone, desert rose selenite.

The crystal for the Sacral chakra goes on your tummy, between your hip bones.

SOLAR PLEXUS CHAKRA

Citrine, yellow fluorite, yellow jasper.

The crystal for the Solar Plexus chakra goes between your ribs and your belly button.

HEART CHAKRA

Pink lepidolite, pink smithsonite, rose quartz, malachite, moldavite, moss agate, peridot.

The crystal for the Heart chakra goes in the middle of your chest, near your heart.

THROAT CHAKRA

Angelite, amazonite, aquamarine, kyanite, lapis lazuli.

The crystal for the Throat chakra goes on your throat.

THIRD EYE CHAKRA

Amethyst, charoite, lilac lepidolite, purple fluorite.

The crystal for the Third Eye chakra goes on the middle of your forehead.

CROWN CHAKRA

Clear quartz, moonstone, selenite.

The crystal for the Crown chakra goes right above your head – on the floor or bed.

If you don't have any particular issues, you could pick any of the associated crystals, and use them to cleanse and balance the chakras.

To balance the chakras, lay down on a flat surface and place one palm stone crystal on each corresponding chakra.

Make yourself comfortable, close your eyes, and take eight deep breaths, just like at the start of the meditation practice.

State each crystal and the chakra it balances out loud and feel their energies merge. Visualize yourself surrounded by a spectrum of colours.

Stay in this blissful state for as long as you like, then bring yourself back to the here and now, and make a journal entry of your experience.

CHAPTER

6

MOST COMMONLY USED CRYSTALS

There are plenty of budget-friendly and powerful stones to help you on your healing journey.

In this section you will find the most commonly-used and widely-available crystals.

These have been sorted into colour groups and ordered according to their associated chakras, for ease of use. At the end of the section, you will find common multicoloured and iridescent crystals and their attributes.

You will find information on each crystal's effect on the spiritual and physical planes. These effects occur when the crystal is worn on the body or kept near to the person.

Do not ingest any crystals: they are for external use only. Do not inhale or ingest any crushed crystals, as they often contain carcinogenic elements or elements that will damage your lungs.

Never rely solely on crystals to heal ailments; always consult a doctor and follow their treatment recommendations, and enhance the recommended therapy with the use of crystals.

Most
commonly
used

BLACK

crystals

Black crystals are associated with the Root chakra.

They all are excellent protectors and helpers in starting anew. They help you to ground yourself and to unveil deep knowledge by looking within.

Black crystals help with issues surrounding the digestive system and the lower parts of the body, including the legs.

BLACK OBSIDIAN

This crystal is associated with the zodiac sign Sagittarius, the planet Jupiter and the element fire.

the physical plane

Black obsidian helps with detoxing the body, easing the pain of healing wounds and getting a restful sleep.

the spiritual plane

Black obsidian helps you see things for what they are and removes any rose-tinted glasses you might have on.

Its sharp edges empower you to cut free from negative energy that doesn't serve you any longer. It aids you in recalling memories that need healing and gives you the strength to deal with them.

It is a great crystal for learning new things and understanding new concepts.

BLACK ONYX

This crystal is associated with the zodiac sign Leo, the planet Saturn and the element fire.

the physical plane

Black onyx helps to alleviate menstrual pain and symptoms such as gastrointestinal issues, bloating, back pain, swelling and aches of the joints.

It can also help with eyestrain and even toothache.

the spiritual plane

Black onyx increases inner strength and gives its wearer the courage and confidence to do what is necessary.

If you lack in self-worth or self-confidence, this stone has a gentle energy that will help you develop a healthier view of yourself.

It is an excellent stone for grounding and for setting boundaries.

SMOKY QUARTZ

This crystal is associated with the zodiac sign Scorpio, the planet Saturn and the element earth.

the physical plane

Smoky quartz aids healthy muscle growth and function, including the heart. It detoxifies the body and helps the blood flow. It can also alleviate cramps in the legs.

the spiritual plane

Smoky quartz is a gentle protector, which keeps you grounded in the here and now while you explore the smoky depths of your soul as you practise shadow work.

It helps you to see through the fog and to plan well ahead, thereby enabling you to turn your dreams into reality.

It is never easy to fight for what you believe in, but this crystal can help by increasing your perseverance and self-worth.

BLACK TOURMALINE

This crystal is associated with the zodiac signs Libra, Capricorn, Scorpio and Sagittarius, the planets Jupiter and Venus and the element water.

the physical plane

As with most black stones, black tourmaline is great for detoxing and maintaining a healthy lifestyle. It can also reduce bloating and other stomach and intestinal issues and help the lymphatic system to stay healthy.

the spiritual plane

Black tourmaline is a powerful spiritual
protector. It guards you on astral travel
and while working with the spirit world.

It unblocks stuck energy and opens up a
healthy flow. It also relieves anxiety and
gives you the strength to face your fears.

It is great for battling self-esteem issues,
while also reminding you to remain
humble and grounded.

Most
commonly
used

RED

crystals

Red stones are associated with the Root chakra.

They are very empowering, both physically and spiritually. They aid in rekindling and feeding our passion and our will to live a full life.

Physically, these stones help us with the digestive and reproductive systems.

CARNELIAN

This crystal is associated with the zodiac signs Leo and Virgo, the planet Mars and the element fire.

the physical plane

Carnelian increases physical strength and endurance. It helps to relieve issues with the blood circulation and the body's overall health.

the spiritual plane

Carnelian lights a spark in you and inspires you to take the first steps and keep walking towards your goal.

It gives mental strength and resolution to its wearer to face whatever the future may hold. It helps you to kick bad habits and ushers in acceptance, forgiveness and positive thinking.

RED JASPER

This crystal is associated with the zodiac sign Aries, the planet Mars and the element fire.

the physical plane

Red jasper is beneficial to the bones, joints and circulation. It also helps with detoxing.

the spiritual plane

Red jasper is the stone of entrepreneurs. It bestows vitality and a go-getter attitude while also providing guidance and confidence when making tough decisions and taking calculated risks.

It can help to dispel the fear of failure, particularly in the winter when it can act as a mini Sun and provide a boost of energy.

It aids dream interpretation and reading signs from the other side, and in realizing your true purpose in life.

RHODOCHROSITE

This crystal is associated with the zodiac signs Leo and Scorpio, the planet Mars and the element fire.

the physical plane

Rhodochrosite helps to stabilize thyroid functions and hormonal imbalances. It can alleviate migraines and help with circulatory issues.

the spiritual plane

Rhodochrosite encourages selflessness and devoting yourself to a cause you believe in.

This is the stone of volunteer work and of people who are in the health industry in any capacity.

While it gives the strength to care for others, it also reminds its wearer that self-care is just as important.

Most
commonly
used

ORANGE

crystals

Orange stones are associated with the Sacral chakra.

They help with self-realization, empowerment and finding joy in your true calling. They also aid in the acceptance of yourself and others and encourage setting healthy boundaries.

They help with seeing the silver lining in difficult situations.

AMBER

This stone is associated with the zodiac signs Leo and Aquarius, the Sun and the element earth.

the physical plane

Amber alleviates teething pain in babies – it is often available as a beaded necklace for the little ones.

It can help with kidney and bladder problems and can help to relieve arthritis pains.

the spiritual plane

Amber is the stone of joyful living. It encourages integrity and loyalty, alleviates anxiety and reduces stress.

It helps you to find joy in the mundane and inspires its wearer to be open to the little miracles of life.

It elevates your overall mental health.

SUNSTONE

This crystal is associated with the zodiac sign Leo, the Sun and the element fire.

the physical plane

Sunstone relieves aches and pains, especially due to rheumatism.

It can also help with metabolism and overall vitality.

the spiritual plane

Sunstone is the crystal of giving and being able to receive kindness.

It encourages the feeling of quiet satisfaction with what you have in life.

It also enables spiritual growth through acceptance and trust in the divine.

DESERT ROSE SELENITE

This crystal is associated with the zodiac sign Taurus, the Moon and the element earth.

the physical plane

Although desert rose selenite is not often used to heal physical ailments, some practitioners use it to strengthen bones and joints.

the spiritual plane

Desert rose selenite is the crystal of mindfulness.

It shows you the bright side of life and demonstrates that even in the harshest of environments, beauty can grow.

It encourages positive changes, gratitude and optimistic thoughts for the future.

Most
commonly
used

YELLOW

crystals

Yellow stones are associated with the Solar Plexus chakra.

They help you to explore and express your true, authentic self and fill you with hope for a bright future.

They encourage a joyful life with integrity as your guide, in which you can spread this radiant self-assuredness to those around you.

CITRINE

This crystal is associated with the zodiac signs Leo and Scorpio, the planets Jupiter and Pluto and the elements earth and fire.

the physical plane

Citrine can help with the side-effects of anxiety, such as eating disorders or hair loss.

It also strengthens the immune system, and speeds up the healing process in general.

the spiritual plane

Citrine is the stone of investing in your future. It helps with investing your energy and your money in a safe and conscientious manner.

It helps to plan for the future and take calculated risks. It also helps to battle fear and anxiety, leaving confidence and clarity in their place.

It encourages a positive mindset and is a powerful aid in fighting depression.

YELLOW FLUORITE

This crystal is associated with the zodiac sign Leo, the Sun and the element fire.

the physical plane

Yellow fluorite aids healthy liver function and helps to detox the body and the mind.

the spiritual plane

Yellow fluorite spreads happiness and teamwork. It encourages its user to make permanent, positive changes, look beyond superficial ideas and see what really matters.

It bestows confidence and removes negative or self-destructive behaviours, such as envy, ruts or addictions, replacing them with creativity and a sense of purpose.

YELLOW JASPER

This crystal is associated with the zodiac sign Leo, the Sun and the element earth.

the physical plane

Yellow jasper supports the immune system and helps to keep the body heathy. It can help with motion sickness or travel sickness.

the spiritual plane

Yellow jasper, like its other colour variants, is a protective stone.

It aids travellers on their journeys – whether an actual trip, astral travel or a life-changing event.

It fills its wearer with positivity and high-vibrational energy.

Most
commonly
used

PINK

crystals

Pink stones are associated with the Heart chakra.

They help with emotional healing and love, and they radiate positive energy.

They aid self-acceptance and self-love, while encouraging the same treatment towards others.

PINK LEPIDOLITE

This crystal is associated with the zodiac signs Libra and Pisces, the planet Jupiter and the element water.

the physical plane

Pink lepidolite relieves anxiety and stress and can have a positive effect on sleep troubles. As a result, it can also help to reverse some of their side-effects such as worry lines, hair loss or damaged nails.

the spiritual plane

Pink lepidolite is the crystal of establishing positive thought patterns. It helps to overcome addictions or bad habits.

If you have trouble with intrusive thoughts or other negative thought patterns, this is the crystal for you. It boosts its wearer's mood and helps with concentration, especially through encouraging a more positive train of thought.

If you often have bad dreams, try sleeping with pink lepidolite under your pillow.

PINK SMITHSONITE

This crystal is associated with the zodiac sign Cancer, the Moon and the element water.

the physical plane

Pink smithsonite can help to overcome trauma and anxiety, strengthen the immune system and clear up problems with the sinuses.

the spiritual plane

This charming crystal can help to increase your self-confidence and positively influence how others see you.

It aids teamwork and collaboration in any type of relationship.

It provides clarity and aids your spiritual journey towards enlightenment.

ROSE QUARTZ

This crystal is associated with the zodiac signs Taurus and Libra, the planet Venus and the element water.

the physical plane

Rose quartz aids healthy heart function and can help with conception.

the spiritual plane

Rose quartz is the crystal of kindness and gentle love.

It encourages acceptance and forgiveness towards yourself and others and helps to let go of old hurts.

It opens your heart to love and brings out a childlike curiosity for the world and its wonders.

Most
commonly
used

GREEN

crystals

Green stones are associated with the Heart chakra.

They encourage integrity, openness and trust.

They also encourage growth, both personal and material, and provide you with the courage to be your true self in the face of opposition.

MALACHITE

This crystal is associated with the zodiac signs Scorpio and Capricorn, the planet Venus and the element earth.

the physical plane

Malachite can help to alleviate the symptoms of arthritis.

the spiritual plane

Malachite opens the heart to empathy
and forgiveness.

It aids in receiving spiritual messages and
prophetic dreams and in communicating
with the other side of the veil, especially
with angels and spirit guides.

MOLDAVITE

This crystal is associated with the zodiac signs Scorpio, Sagittarius and Capricorn and the element fire.

Because it is a tektite crystal, meaning it was created by a meteorite crashing into Earth, it is not connected to a single heavenly body, but rather to the whole cosmos.

the physical plane

Moldavite can help to detoxify the body and aid healthy heart functioning.

the spiritual plane

Moldavite is the embodiment of tough love. It ushers in drastic spiritual and personal change and growth, so caution must be used when working with this stone. You must be mentally and emotionally prepared for the journey that this stone will take you on, and trust that you will come out whole and new on the other side.

By opening up the flow of energy through your chakras, it makes you resistant to negative situations and prepares you to change them for the better. It also opens all windows of communication with higher realms, so it is perfect to strengthen your spiritual gifts.

MOSS AGATE

This crystal is associated with the zodiac sign Virgo, the planet Earth and the element earth.

the physical plane

Moss agate speeds up healing. It encourages healthy growth and helps to repair the skin and nails.

the spiritual plane

Moss agate is the crystal of nature.
It is nurturing, grounding and brings
abundance in your life.

It encourages growth and creativity to
help build and enhance your life.

It aids the growth of plants, so it is a
great stone for gardeners, even if you
only have the one house plant.

PERIDOT

This crystal is associated with the zodiac sign Leo, the Sun and the elements fire and earth.

the physical plane

Peridot promotes overall physical wellbeing.

the spiritual plane

Peridot is a powerful protector of the heart.

It guards against those who would use you and helps you see them for who they truly are.

It protects against gossip and verbal abuse, wards off nightmares and alleviates the pain of loss.

Most
commonly
used

BLUE and
TURQUOISE

crystals

Blue and turquoise stones are associated with the Throat chakra.

They help with clarity, communication and self-expression. They help to further strengthen your emotional intelligence and encourage truthfulness and integrity.

Blue stones are also connected to the Third Eye chakra, which helps you to view things as they truly are and see things that are not visible to the naked eye. They also aid in developing psychic abilities.

ANGELITE

This crystal is associated with the zodiac sign Aquarius, the planet Uranus and the element air.

the physical plane

Angelite relieves tension headaches and issues around the throat and neck area.

the spiritual plane

Angelite promotes your communication skills, especially on a spiritual level: it facilitates psychic abilities by energetically connecting you to angelic realms.

It increases intuition, empathy and compassion.

AMAZONITE

This crystal is associated with the zodiac sign Virgo, the planet Uranus and the element water.

the physical plane

Amazonite promotes overall physical wellness. It is beneficial for the throat and oral cavity and promotes better absorption of calcium.

the spiritual plane

Amazonite is a great crystal to help you to establish assertiveness and set and enforce boundaries.

It promotes clear communication and determination, and it relieves stress by helping to reduce triggers caused by miscommunication.

It helps you to see people for who they are, aiding you in choosing better friends, spouses and business partners.

AQUAMARINE

This crystal is associated with the zodiac signs Pisces and Aries, the Moon and the element water.

the physical plane

Aquamarine relieves travel sickness, calms the mind and can help with water retention in the body.

the spiritual plane

Aquamarine enhances self-confidence and boosts your inner strength.

It works by helping you to see things from a different perspective: if things seem difficult, it teaches you that life is a journey and lessons can be learned from all the hardships, especially lessons that help to turn a negative situation into a positive one.

KYANITE

This crystal is associated with the zodiac signs Libra, Taurus and Aries, the planet Venus and the element air.

the physical plane

Kyanite enhances overall bodily health, especially around the throat. It helps to repair and maintain muscles.

the spiritual plane

Kyanite enhances your skills in dream work and spiritual practices, especially communication with the other side.

It helps you to forgive and leave resentment behind. It encourages open, honest communication with everyone.

LAPIS LAZULI

This crystal is associated with the zodiac sign Sagittarius, the planet Jupiter and the element water.

the physical plane

Lapis lazuli can help you to view your purpose clearly. By doing so, it relieves depression and fills you with hope for the future.

Because it promotes actively going after your dreams, it relieves sleep related problems as well.

the spiritual plane

Lapis lazuli is the crystal of psychics. It enhances your connection to the spirit world, strengthens intuition, clairvoyance and other clair-abilities, prophetic dreams and everything that is magical.

It provides powerful protection against evil forces while practicing magic, and raises the body's vibrations.

It is one of the most powerful stones, so you might need a little time to get used to it.

Most
commonly
used

PURPLE
and VIOLET

crystals

Purple crystals are associated with the Third Eye chakra.

They open your eyes to realms beyond our own and increase intuition and psychic abilities.

They encourage connection to the spirit world, looking inwards and discovering your true self and letting go of the material world.

AMETHYST

This crystal is associated with the zodiac signs Pisces, Virgo, Aquarius and Capricorn, the planet Jupiter and the element air.

the physical plane

Amethyst alleviates stress and issues with sleep and promotes an overall sense of wellbeing.

the spiritual plane

Amethyst is the crystal of peace, one of the gentlest stones in any healer's toolkit.

It balances emotions, grounds you in the present while relieving grief and also soothes the soul.

It reinforces your resolution and inner strength.

CHAROITE

This crystal is associated with the zodiac sign
Scorpio, the planet Venus and the element
water.

the physical plane

Charoite promotes good eye health and
relieves headaches and stress.

the spiritual plane

Charoite is the crystal of perception. It helps you to see things for what they are and understand why they are that way.

It helps you to heal addictions and obsessive behaviours by encouraging shadow work and curing the root cause of these behaviours.

LILAC LEPIDOLITE

This crystal is associated with the zodiac signs Libra and Pisces, the planet Jupiter and the element water.

the physical plane

Lilac lepidolite helps to establish a good immune system and relieves stress.

the spiritual plane

Lilac lepidolite provides clarity and helps to establish your priorities, be they at work or in life in general.

It aids decision making and researching and reminds you not to give in to impulsive reactions to unexpected hurdles.

It can help with overcoming possessiveness and hoarding by revealing what is truly important.

PURPLE FLUORITE

This crystal is associated with the zodiac signs Pisces and Capricorn, the planet Neptune and the element air.

the physical plane

Purple fluorite relieves stress and its physical manifestations, such as skin problems, hair loss, broken nails and insomnia.

the spiritual plane

Purple fluorite enhances psychic gifts and protects against negative entities.

It can unblock the flow of energy in the body and the chakra system, and it amplifies the effect of other crystals.

Most
commonly
used

WHITE
and CLEAR

crystals

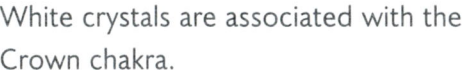

White crystals are associated with the Crown chakra.

They open your consciousness to higher realms, enable you to see your true calling and help you to discover your higher self.

They show you the way out of the dark night of the soul and strengthen your bond with your true tribe and kin.

CLEAR QUARTZ

This crystal is associated with all zodiac signs, the Moon and the element air.

the physical plane

Clear quartz strengthens the immune system and relieves stress and anxiety.

the spiritual plane

Clear quartz amplifies the energy of any other crystal you are working with.

On its own, it opens your eyes to see beyond the surface, in both the physical and spiritual worlds.

It opens the mind to new information and possibilities and cleanses your aura.

MOONSTONE

This crystal is associated with the zodiac sign Cancer, the Moon and the element water.

the physical plane

Moonstone is the go-to crystal for anyone who menstruates or is experiencing the menopause.

It relieves menstrual pain and symptoms of the menopause, including mood swings and temperature changes.

the spiritual plane

Moonstone calms the mind and the
nerves. It reveals and strengthens psychic
abilities, such as intuition, clairvoyance
and dream work.

It calms the heart and opens it up to
giving and receiving love.

It keeps away bad dreams and manifests
a good night's sleep.

SELENITE

This crystal is associated with the zodiac sign Taurus, the Moon and the element air.

the physical plane

Selenite aids metabolism, especially the absorption of nutrients. Through this, it also improves the sleep, hair and skin of its user.

the spiritual plane

Selenite is the crystal of purity. It cleanses other crystals, magical tools – such as tarot cards – and the body's energy system.

As a guardian crystal, it keeps away negative spirits and enhances any magical activity.

It cleanses the mind and heart and eases the process of forgiveness and reconciliation.

Most
commonly
used

MULTI-
COLOURED

crystals

Multi-coloured crystals are usually associated with the chakra that corresponds to their main colour.

In addition to their main healing properties, they also carry the power of their secondary colours.

This makes multicoloured crystals especially useful, as they can connect with multiple chakras at once and can therefore provide many different types of healing.

BLOODSTONE

This crystal is associated with the zodiac signs Aries and Pisces, the planet Mars, the element earth and the Root chakra.

the physical plane

It helps with infections and cleansing the blood. It can also help to improve the quality of blood.

the spiritual plane

Bloodstone is the crystal of rational thinking. It promotes creativity while keeping your grounded.

It enhances intuition, especially through grounding this skill in reality and not letting your fantasy run away with you.

It also helps you to analyze dreams.

LABRADORITE

This crystal is associated with the zodiac signs Leo, Scorpio and Sagittarius, the planet Uranus, the element water and the Third Eye chakra.

the physical plane

Labradorite can relieve headaches and eyestrain. It can also help with brain-related diseases and disorders.

the spiritual plane

Labradorite is one of the strongest crystals for psychics. It opens and balances the Third Eye chakra, helping you to discover and strengthen your abilities.

It makes you more receptive to messages and signs, especially in dreams. It aids lucid dreaming.

TIGER'S EYE

This crystal is associated with the zodiac
signs Gemini, Leo and Capricorn, the planet
Mars, the element fire and the Solar Plexus
chakra.

the physical plane

Tiger's eye helps with eye-related problems.
It is also beneficial for the spine and
promotes healthy muscles.

the spiritual plane

Tiger's eye is the crystal of vibrant vitality. It endows its user with optimism, a healthy self-esteem and resilience in the face of hardship.

It strengthens your resilience and keeps away negative influences.

TURRITELLA AGATE

This crystal is associated with the zodiac signs Taurus and Gemini, the planet Earth, the element of earth and the Root chakra.

the physical plane

Turritella agate helps to maintain overall health, especially of the blood and the bones.

the spiritual plane

Turritella agate is the crystal of connecting with nature and your deepest thoughts and feelings.

It aids shamanic journeys and past-life regressions.

It also helps you to heal from and overcome traumatic events and access old memories.

UNAKITE

This crystal is associated with the zodiac signs Scorpio and Cancer, the planet Mars, the element of earth and the Heart chakra.

the physical plane

Unakite aids healing in all areas of the body and aids the healthy functioning of the respiratory system, the heart and the blood vessels.

the spiritual plane

Unakite induces gentle, gradual change. It provides you with the endurance to strive for a better future and helps you to discover the root of any problems that you might face.

It opens the heart to growth and forgiveness, compassion and understanding of yourself and others.

CHAPTER

7

CRYSTAL COMBINATIONS for SPECIFIC AILMENTS

It would be impossible to list all the ailments a person might have over their lifetime, but this list has some of the most common problems that you might experience. For a personalized crystal treatment, it is best to contact a certified crystal healer.

Use these crystal combinations with any techniques listed in this book. Make grids, prepare potions, meditate with or wear these crystals to aid the treatment of your issue.

Remember, all this is in addition to any treatment your medical professional has prescribed for you.

addictions and bad habits

- **black tourmaline** for protection, detoxification and letting go.

- **smoky quartz** for cleansing, health and strength.

- **citrine** for motivation and healing skin concerns, such as eczema.

- **agate** for healing the skin.

balancing blood pressure

- **amethyst** for stress relief and peace.

- **rose quartz** for healthy heart functioning.

- **peridot** for balancing the Heart chakra.

colds, flu and coughs

- **pink smithsonite** for boosting the immune system and clearing the sinuses.

- **carnelian** for energy and strength.

- **aquamarine** for clearing up a blocked nose and phlegm from the throat.

depression

- **moss agate** for balancing emotions and healing.

- **yellow fluorite** for healing, positive thoughts and being able to accept help.

- **lapis lazuli** for seeing a brighter future and finding hope.

grief

- **amethyst** for emotional peace.
- **rose quartz** for soothing emotions.
- **black obsidian** for grounding and to enable healing.

hair loss

- **moonstone** for stimulating hair growth and clearing toxins.
- **unakite** for stimulating blood flow to the scalp.

headaches

- **labradorite** for reducing head pain.

- **amethyst** for tiredness and stress relief.

- **angelite** for relieving pain.

period pain:

- **noonstone** for calming emotions and relieving pain.

- **carnelian** for easing pain and regulating the flow.

sprains, strains and muscle pains

- **turquoise** for aiding tissue repair.

- **kyanite** for strengthening muscles.

- **carnelian** for energy.

eye strain

- **tiger's eye** for soothing the eye and restoring its vitality.

- **amethyst** for relieving strain on the eyes.

With all the information provided, you can begin your journey down the path of crystal healing.

Remember to breathe, remain open to receiving and stay true to yourself.

Blessed be!